Machines at Work

Garbage Trucks

by Cari Meister

Bullfrog Books

Ideas for Parents and Teachers

Bullfrog Books let children practice nonfiction reading at the earliest reading levels. Repetition, familiar words, and photo labels support early readers.

Before Reading

- Discuss the cover photo. What does it tell them?
- Look at the picture glossary together. Read and discuss the words.

Read the Book

- "Walk" through the book and look at the photos. Let the child ask questions. Point out the photo labels.
- Read the book to the child, or have him or her read independently.

After Reading

- Prompt the child to think more. Ask: What kind of garbage truck collects your trash? How does it work?

Bullfrog Books are published by Jump!
5357 Penn Avenue South
Minneapolis, MN 55419
www.jumplibrary.com

Library of Congress Cataloging-in-Publication Data
Meister, Cari.
  Garbage trucks / by Cari Meister.
    pages cm. -- (Bullfrog books. Machines at work)
  Includes bibliographical references and index.
  Summary: "This photo-illustrated book for early readers tells about the parts of a garbage truck and different kinds of trucks used to collect trash"-- Provided by publisher.
  Audience: Grades K to grade 3.
  ISBN 978-1-62031-045-8 (hardcover : alk. paper) -- ISBN 978-1-62496-057-4 (ebook)
  1. Refuse collection vehicles--Juvenile literature. 2. Refuse and refuse disposal--Juvenile literature. I. Title.
  TD794.M45 2014
  628.4'42--dc23
                                    2012042017

Series Editor: Rebecca Glaser
Book Editor: Patrick Perish
Series Designer: Ellen Huber

Photo Credits:
Dreamstime, 4, 5, 13, 15, 17, 18, 22(main), 23ml, 23tr, 23mr, 22br; Getty, 8, 14, 23bl; iStock, 21, 24; Shutterstock, 1, 3 (both), 6, 7, 9, 10, 12, 22bl, 23tl, 23br; Superstock, cover, 3, 11

Printed in the United States of America at Corporate Graphics in North Mankato, Minnesota.
5-2013 / PO 1003
10 9 8 7 6 5 4 3 2 1

Table of Contents

Garbage Trucks at Work

Screech!
The garbage truck stops.
It is trash day.

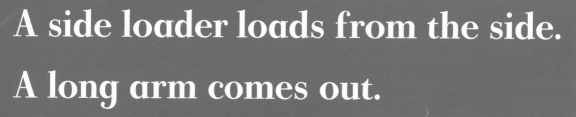

6

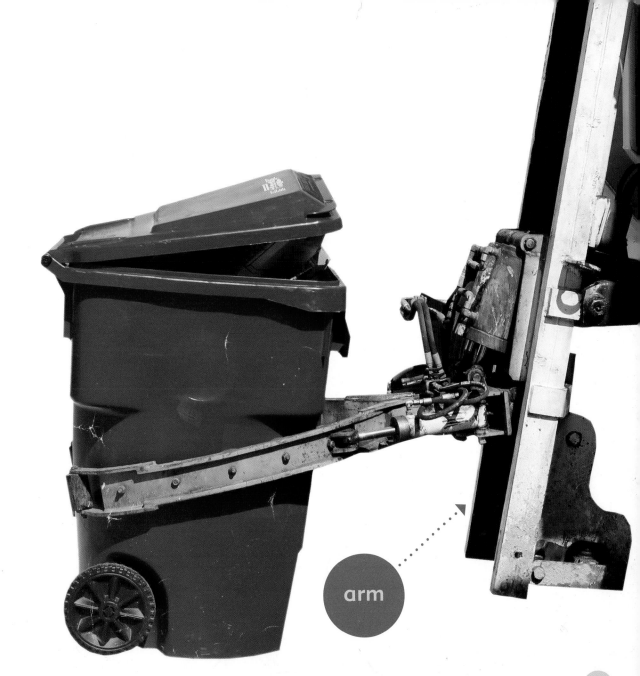

arm

The driver uses a joystick.
It moves the arm to grab the can.

Up, up goes the can.

joystick········· ▶

Whoosh!
The can tilts.

Trash falls.

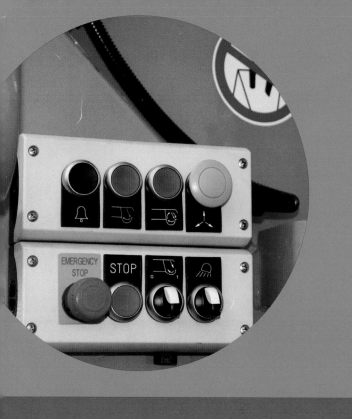

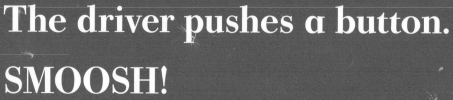

The driver pushes a button.

SMOOSH!

The crusher blade presses down the bags.

crusher
blade

Watch out!

Here comes a front loader.

14

forks

It has forks.

They lift heavy dumpsters.

Beep! Beep!

Rear loaders collect garbage in the back.

Workers put trash in the hopper.

hopper

The truck is full.
It needs to dump.
Where does it go?
The landfill!
The truck dumps.

18

Vroom!

Off it goes.

Time to get more trash.

Parts of a Garbage Truck

hopper
A space in a garbage truck where the garbage is kept until it is dumped.

joystick
A lever used to control the arm.

crusher blade
A heavy metal blade that smashes garbage.

Picture Glossary

dumpster
A large container for trash.

landfill
A large area where garbage is buried.

forks
Two long metal pieces on the front of a truck that lift heavy things.

rear loader
A garbage truck where the trash is loaded from the back.

front loader
A garbage truck with forks on the front that lifts dumpsters.

side loader
A garbage truck where the trash is collected on the side with a robotic arm.

Index

To Learn More

Learning more is as easy as 1, 2, 3.

1) Go to www.factsurfer.com

2) Enter "garbage truck" into the search box.

3) Click the "Surf" button to see a list of websites.

With factsurfer.com, finding more information is just a click away.

24